MOORISH AMERICAN
CIVICS GUIDE

"The strength of a nation derives from the integrity of the home." ~ Prophet Confucius

Prepared and compiled by:

Sheik Way-El

www.moorishsciencetemple.org

MOORISH AMERICAN CIVICS GUIDE

By Sheik Way El, MOORISH SCIENCE TEMPLE OF AMERICA©

First edition – published 2014

Lulu Publishing

ISBN: 978-1-312-77715-6

Printed in the United States of America

Prophet Noble Drew Ali Founder of the Moorish Science Temple of America, the Moorish Divine and National Movement for the uplifting of fallen humanity

Table of Contents

Preface

The purpose of this monograph is to emphasize the importance of instruction in citizenship among the members of the Moorish Science Temple of America. The brief discussions of the several phases of the subject and of the methods of teaching it are sufficient to give the member the modern social point of view and to awaken an enthusiasm for the subject which is lacking among the disenfranchised Moors on this land branded under the false color-coded labels of Negro, Black, Colored, and African American.

The course of studying civics given at the close of the treatise is intended as a guide to the teacher in the selection of life-units for the instruction and training of the Moorish American Moslems, more specifically to our young boys and girls in active citizenship. The fundamental principle of co-operation in group life for the mutual welfare of all citizens is made prominent throughout the course.

These simple lessons are to lead the teacher and student into broader lessons and applications as it pertains to American life. If you think about it, our people have never truly enjoyed the American life because they were operating off of privileges as opposed to the God given rights conferred to all citizens under the constitution of a free national government. For the first time in decades, our people, the Moorish American Moslems, will be taught those things necessary so that they can become better citizens of this great nation. One can only attain power in this nation by sitting in the seats where the powerful sit. In order to do this, one must properly be taught the civic side of the American life, something that has never been properly taught to all the people of Moorish descent in this nation.

In these modern days, it is the mission of the Moorish Science Temple of America to bring the civic understanding of American life, from the Moorish American Moslem perspective, who is in fact a part and a partial to this government of the United States of America.

This civics guide is designed to awaken you as to how a government is run and how citizens of that government operate in turn to make it run. We Moabites, or Moors, are the founders of the world's first civilizations and what we have among the nations today are modifications of the very civility that was bred by the high types of our ancient societies. We pray Allah this book finds you in good spirits and you apply the information therein for the betterment of yourself, your household, your family, your community, and your nation in general. Peace.

1. Civics and Citizenship

A. What Civics Is

Civics teaches people how to be good citizens in group life, such as the family, the school, the city, and the state. It deals with topics such as manners, obedience, duty, industry, protection of life, health and property, the payment of taxes and rents, the work of the community, of officials, of the courts, of legislatures, congress, political parties, fraternal, and patriotic organizations.

This subject places emphasis upon relationships between individuals in a group and between groups of individuals in their efforts to deal with and to serve one another. In other words, civics is the subject that treats of the co-operative relations of individuals and groups in their attempts to live and work together. It pertains to the life of children as well as to the life of adults. For these reasons it is one of the most important subjects for a Moorish American Moslem to study as it is they, falsely and formerly called by the slave epithets Negro, Black, and Colored, who have fallen away from this form of civilized life due to never having a proper education and understanding of what this life entails.

B. Why Civics Should Be Taught

An examination of the courses of study in typical neighborhoods called "ghettos" throughout the country reveals the fact that not very much attention is given to this subject in a serious or systematic way; whether it be in the daily program of the schools, Temples, Churches, Mosques, religious organizations or other organizations in general.

This is doubtless due to the fact that in past years, civics has been regarded as a formal text-book subject, dealing with the machinery of government and suited only to the upper echelon of American society and taught within their upper grammar grades and the high school, as preparation for adult citizenship. Since the advent of the Moorish Science Temple of America and its recent resurgence, this viewpoint has changed. The organization of the Moorish Science Temple of America is akin to this American civic temperament in its aims, methods and subject matter. Prophet Noble Drew Ali realized that in order to infuse the disenfranchised Moors here who were branded with the slave labels of Negro, blacks, coloreds (and today's *African American*), that a greater effort had to be made through the Temples to supply the members and more specifically, the children with the ideas and the activities that result in habits of conduct and habits of service befitting a co-operative social, political and industrial life. Children come to understand the more remote and more complex phases of life through an understanding of and an interest in the concrete activities of their daily human relationships. This puts civics, the subject that treats of these relationships, in the program of every aspect of the course of Islamism and its study in its cooperative understanding of the Divine and National dichotomy of this Movement. Before Prophet Noble Drew Ali brought this civic awareness to the masses of our people in the city of Chicago, the disconnect was wedged and the people were mistreated and scattered and so the necessity for this civic training was not strongly felt, but now that people are awaking and beginning to realize that the Prophet is the source of light in America and is the acorn that grew the great oak tree that has many branches in the form of a variety of organization, the pressure for a harmonious and stimulating conception and control of human relationships is growing greater day by day.

The ever increasing difficulties of maintaining peaceful international relationships call for a higher type of world citizenship and a new interpretation of patriotism. Love of humanity must transcend love of country in this new citizenship ideal, if the people of the world are to succeed in living together in unison, as advanced technology and increasing population is placing them. Prophet Noble Drew Ali emphasized this love because when one adheres to the principles of love first and foremost, then he/she will be the most productive member of society. On several of occasions we see where the Prophet stated:

> *"The heads of all Temples, Grand Sheiks, Grand Sheikess must confirm to the Divine principles: Love, Truth, Peace, Freedom, and Justice. They must live the life among the members and be loved even as the Prophet is loved…They must live the life of Love, Truth, Peace, Freedom, and Justice…Adhere at all times to the principles of love, truth, peace, freedom, and justice…Our Divine and National Movement stands for the specific grand principles of Love, Truth, Peace, Freedom, and Justice… We are for Love, Truth, Peace, Freedom, and Justice, and when these principles are violated, justice must then take its course."*

The public school was once thought of as being a striking illustration of this new community life as the school was supposed to be the center of all phases of child and adult life the year around. Unfortunately, the public school system has failed a majority of our people as it does not teach the vitally needed use of the moral compass and how to use such to navigate for the rest of their lives. For this, a civic education was introduced to us by Prophet Noble Drew Ali and has since been long suppressed by other organizations that came after. Another illustration is the consolidation and federation of religious institutions built upon peace advances to the human race, both at home and in the foreign fields, for the strengthening of the feeling of oneness of human interests and the breaking down of the unreal and artificial differences between mankind. Nothing expressed this point like Mohammedan Islam which united scattered societies and cultures into one force. Unfortunately, even that form of Islam produced men who altered the meanings of texts to fit their own delusions of how the world should be and so Allah sent us a universal Prophet, Noble Drew Ali, with a universal message and he taught *"Love, Truth, Peace, Freedom, and Justice which alone can save the nations."*

Individuals, as such, and as members of religious organizations and social groups should make civics instruction necessary in every grade of learning. An analogy of this is found in the religious training of children in the home and the place of worship where the efforts of the parents and religious teachers are unceasing. The child, as it enters school and passes from grade to grade, is conscious of its duties to others and of its blessings from others when the proper civic instructions are taught and enforced on a daily basis.

It also sees the necessity of modifying its habits and notions regarding right and wrong as its interests and relationships widen. In these newer and richer experiences he/she needs not only the environment that calls forth and necessitates the changes, but also the sympathetic and intelligent guidance of those directing his/her fuller training.

The gradation in the child's development is paralleled by the grades in the school (or home school) and should be met grade by grade with more intensive study of the lessons begun in the lower grades coupled with new interests. Learning from environment alone is not enough; the teacher must help the child to organize its reactions upon this environment so as to make more certain a wholesome interest and a social attitude. The gradation of the work in classes from primary to the higher grades should be from an observation of the services rendered by one individual to another, upward through the social groups and institutions to the machinery of government as a means of conducting, controlling and advancing all individual and social activities.

At every step of the way, emphasis must be put upon helpful human service, as the fundamental principle of true citizenship. The message of the Moorish Science Temple of America should be a constant reminder to all students of the field and all members in general:

> "We are friends and servants of humanity. We are dedicated to the purpose of elevating the moral, social, and economic status of our people. We have set about to do this through a wide and comprehensive program embodying the principles of love, truth, peace, freedom, and justice."

C. Citizenship—Its True Meaning

A new conception prevails today of the citizen and citizenship. The narrowness of the Egyptian city-state is deep buried in the past; the suzerainty of the Moorish government in Spain was dissipated by the virility of the envious Nations of European monarchs; the divinely appointed king ruling over the rest of us as subjects now sleeps peacefully; lords and serfs today dine together; capitalists and laborers look for protection to the same courts; rival nations are dreaming of a universal board of arbitration; one language, through trained interpreters, tells these tales of progress the world around; the World Wide Web (internet), by relays, encircles the earth with a message of man's triumphs and eminent failures. These changed conditions make a new world and necessitates a new type of citizenship. The nations of the earth are closer together today than the Egyptian States were thousands of years ago. All kind of commercial, political and social relations among the nations makes each nation dependent upon each other more so now than we ever have seen according to recorded history. These ties call for a citizenship and patriotism free from race antagonisms and illumined with the spirit of human service and we feel that the very tenets of the Moorish American doctrine, descendants of the world's first civilization and divine creed, can bring this very ideal to fruition.

The means of education have so multiplied through the internet and the press that the people of the world can no longer be kept in ignorance of what the world offers to the enlightened.

Every citizen of a free country aspires to read and think for him or herself, to vote and to have a voice in shaping every institution of society. We are fed, clothed, and entertained from every land and every clime and we traverse the world over for pleasure, knowledge and wealth. All of these privileges and blessings are brought to our homes and shared with our children. The lives of children and adults day by day are enriched from the treasure-stores of the world. The morning, noon, and evening press relays to us of the struggles, conquests, sorrows, and joys of mankind everywhere. The new citizenship means a preparation for the understanding and appreciation of this complex and rich world-life. The leading nations are all engaged in this progressive development of civilization. The echoes of war are but accidents in this forward march of humanity. The Moorish American Moslems must now take their places at the table and engage once again, in the affairs of men.

The peoples of the world understand each other better and are more deeply concerned with their mutual welfare than ever before. The proper education of our children for the further development of this spirit and work is the most vital cause in which society can engage.

D. Specific Aims in Teaching Civics

Besides our moral and spiritual growth, civics is as rich in specific aims as any other subject of the Moorish American curriculum. These aims are even more vital in the development of real men and women than are the aims of other subjects. In fact, the highest aims of all the subjects of the curriculum are the ones whose blossom and fruitage is citizenship.

i. Reverence for the home is fundamental in the training of children. The ceaseless grind of the unhallowed child support and divorce courts attests this need. The family and the home of the family is the unit for civilization. No virtue is needed, or in fact can be, in any other social, political, or industrial group that is not essential to a pure and efficient home. Patience, sympathy, duty, service, obedience, honesty, truthfulness, courage, fortitude, industry, sacrifice, forgiveness, purity,—are not all of these the virtues of a righteous home? Do all children receive sufficient training in these virtues in their home? The first duty of the Temple (or home) school is to supplement the work of the home in developing in the children the habits and attitudes which underlie the character of a true citizen. Children not reared in a spirit of reverence for the home—the institution that brought them into existence—are but poorly equipped to enter into the broader relationships of life in which the home is but a unit. This begs repeating the quote from Prophet Confucius in the opening page of this book; *"The strength of a nation derives from the integrity of the home."*

Virtues are not acquired by merely passing over the boundary line from one institution into another—they must become bone and sinew of the individual and this is where the Divine Instructions given us by our Prophet Noble Drew Ali in our Moorish Holy Koran is of the utmost importance.

ii.   Learning to share with one another our blessings is an aim in our newfound citizenship. The child especially needs to learn early and well the lesson that no one can live his life alone and that he enjoys no blessing to which others have not made a contribution. The home is protected from fire and from the robber by the organized service of the individuals of society. The public school that the child attends is maintained by a common tax or the Temple's (or other religious organization) school is maintained by donations from the common citizen alike.

Likewise the Temple, Mosque, Church, the library, the parks, the roads—these are made possible by a sharing of service. The good citizen makes his contribution to the common welfare. More and more society is expecting this mutual service from her members—both from the poor and from the rich. The idea today is that the good citizen is the one who holds an opportunity or wealth only as a trustee to use it for the common good. He is not a parasite, living without working, but is a producer of wealth; he is not a miser (cheapskate), hoarding his income, but is a distributor of his goods. With this point of view, that individual or that nation which creates and distributes the most to the peoples of the world is the best and greatest in citizenship. The Temple and the school connected thereof, in all of its teachings and activities should give the children this point of view. This is the thought in the Preamble to the United States Constitution, *"to promote the common welfare and to secure the blessings of liberty to ourselves and to our posterity."*

The child in its simplicity will catch this spirit if it is the tone and the teaching of the home and the school.

iii.   Citizens should be able to make the wisest selections of vocations, and should see, appreciate, and do what society needs. At this point, the present-day training for citizenship is weak. But little is being done systematically to help the boys and girls, regardless of national descent, to discover what they are best fitted to do and to help them to analyze the needs of society in the various industries and professions. And society is not doing enough in an unselfish way to aid young people in entering upon their vocations with assurance of success.

Prophet Noble Drew Ali spoke to this civic duty in the form of encouragement and support of business ventures sought and established by Moorish American Moslems and by urging those of us who have been accustomed to criticizing our own people, to cease such action as this is a backwards action that degrades any society. He stated:

> "Our men, women and children should be taught to believe in the capacity of our group to succeed in business, in spite of the trials and failures of some of them. Trials and failures in business are by no means confined to any particular group of people. Some business ventures of all people fail. We have many men and women among our people who are qualified, both by training and experience, who are shining lights in the business world of all the people. It is a sad weakness in us as a people that we have withheld the very encouragement, support and patronage that would have made some of our worthy business ventures a grand success. And worst of all, have joined in the condemnations of them when they failed."

It is reliably stated that less than one fifth of our people are successful financially. This means a large percentage of dissatisfied and inefficient people—a type of citizenship that creates problems difficult to solve. To admit that this condition cannot be remedied however, is to place a low estimate upon the business ability of humanity and a low estimate upon the ability of the one-fifth as teachers of the four-fifths. If it is possible to turn the millions consumed in war and other nonproductive enterprises, especially those of Moorish descent, into helping the young to choose the right vocation and to get started right in it, thereby many of the social problems would be solved. Several of the leading countries and many cities in the United States are doing valuable work in vocational directing. Unfortunately, these works are usually confined to the more privileged in society when it comes to the United States of America and the inner cities are blocked off from such light from failure to see any other options other than the ones they believe that they are limited to.

To contrast, places like India will produce a crop of fifteen year olds who are ready to move on to become surgeons and doctors and overall masters in the medical fields. Such should be the mindset of the Moorish Americans who are falsely mislabeled by the slave labels of "Black" within this nation. "Ghettoes" as they are called in this nation, can, in an instant be turned into beacons of civic engagement and vocational training ripened to do business within this nation and other nations as they establish businesses on American soils. Couple that with an informed electorate and in one generation, the whole race would be resurrected from its economic and civil futility.

The goal in citizenship should be, every citizen at the work for which he is best fitted and meeting with success in that work. If this directing is to be done through the Temple's schools, then this means that our schools ought to be the very center and heart-beat of our nation. The work is too big for an individual or for private enterprise; it must be done by society as a whole through a universal institution. We have but one such institution and that is the Moorish Science Temple of America. A sad refrain is heard on every hand, *"If I had only known where to go at when I was a youngster."* If our society and society in general can remedy this condition through the right kind of education and direction of her youth, charity houses, jails, and penitentiaries will close automatically. A large percentage of lawyers, doctors and tradesmen might, with profit to society, be turned into vocational directors for the young.

iv. Citizens should protect their nation, but not destroy others. The policy of live and let live, applied to the individuals in our home, should be applicable, in the same sense and equally so, to the nations of the earth. It will be so if the human consciousness ever expands sufficiently to grasp the idea of Love, Truth, Peace, Freedom and Justice being practiced in all the nations of the earth bringing about a world citizenship. If our youth grow up with the idea that it is only the best to which they are to be true, and that imaginary geographical boundary lines do not sever truth and human interests, then the love of one's own nation or country will not be despoiled by the hatred of other nations. The doctrine of *"God bless the United States of America"* without asking the same God to bless the other nations of the earth equally, has no place in the mental framework of a truly civilized society. The citizens of any country should be prepared—abundantly prepared for defense against any foe, but the bulwarks of their defense should be the virtues of a righteous nation. These may justly be manned by the military might of a nation respectfully. Any other means of national defense is but for a day. When a citizen of one country sees justice in the claim of a citizen of another country, then he must become the protector of his fellow citizen. It is in this sense that citizenship transcends boundary lines and nations are kept at peace.

The child can understand this principle via his/her Temple school and community relationships, if he/she be guided by one who sees the end of it all.

v. Citizens should understand and know how to enjoy the best in work and leisure. The riches of a civilization are of no consequence except as they are understood and used.

The wealth of literature, art and science are like the mines in the earth until revealed to the minds of men. The contributions made by the earlier peoples make life richer both in service and enjoyment if properly interpreted. We need to know how other people have lived, thought, and governed themselves in order to fully appreciate our own conditions and to know whether to repeat or to avoid their manner of life. This is a duty of an intelligent citizen.

All civilizations borrowed from other civilizations so the thought that Moors should gloat about being the first civilization and that all other civilizations stole their knowledge of civilization from us is backwards and asinine. Being the first people to bring civilization as a light to the world, then that duty should remain the priority of any civilized nation to help develop a people who may be in any way uncivilized and unaware of that condition.

Likewise a helpful use of leisure hours calls for a wide knowledge and careful training. The lack of this fills the clubs and party scene, gambling halls, the bar, and the loafing dens with aimless, disintegrating characters that become a tumor on the society in general.

The remedy lies in appreciation of literature, art, music, healthful games, social amusements, positive motion-pictures, and public parks. The schools are developing these activities very extensively and society is realizing the value of it as redeeming and preventive factors in education. Such work is emphasizing the fact that training for citizenship is much more than mere preparation to vote and to make laws. An intelligent laborer in a wisely chosen vocation with wholesome leisure hours is the highest product of any civilization. Chapter 29 vv. 3-10 teaches us:

> "The glory of a king is the welfare of his people; his power and dominion rest on the hearts of his subjects. The mind of a great prince is exalted with the grandeur of his situation; he advances high things, and searches for business worthy of his power. He summons together the wise men of his kingdom; he consuls among them with freedom, and hears the opinions of them all. He looks amongst his people with discernment; he discovers the abilities of men, and employs them each according to their merits. His magistrates are just, his ministers are wise, and the favorite of his bosom would never deceive him. He smiles upon the arts, and they flourish; the sciences improve beneath the culture of his hand. He delights himself with the learned and ingenious; he sparks in their breasts emulation; and the glory of his kingdom is exalted by their labors. The spirit of the merchant who extends his commerce, the skill of the farmer who enriches his lands, the ingenuity of the artists, the improvements of the scholar; all these he honors with his favor, or rewards with his bounty."

The Holy Koran of the Moorish Science Temple of America provides us with the framework of a civilized society governed by reason, logic, and discernment, but more important, morals and virtues.

vi.   The practice of civic virtues and the appreciation of rights and duties is a constant aim of all instructed in civics.

It is the individual in service, with a happy heart and a moral will, guided by a social conscience that draws the blueprint for this new level of educational reform. The child must learn that his right to life, liberty, property, and joy is coupled with a duty to secure and preserve the same right to every other individual. The home, Temple, school, and community are full of opportunities and necessities for the practice of this virtue. In these phases of group life, in which the child is participating, example counts for more than precept. Here the habit is formed that makes a good citizen. A person must be the message that they bring.

vii.   Knowledge of the organization and administration of the machinery of the government is necessary for the fullest conception of the functions of its several parts.

The machinery of government is of no value aside from what it does for society. The citizen needs to know how this machine operates so that he/she may use it to bring to pass desired social results. He should be taught to think of it not as something either sacred or fixed, but as something that can and must change as human needs change. In this regard only must the citizen respect government, officials, laws, and courts. Good citizens make good government.

viii.   A supreme aim in the teaching of civics is to prepare citizens to meet and destroy the efforts of organized vice.

On every hand, in life about us, is found organized vice, luring our boys and girls and adult citizens away from the path of righteousness. Illustrations are the drug dealer and the drug user, music that glorifies the latter; the club/party scene, the bar, the gambling spots, the traffic in women, the corrupt methods in business practices, etc.

All of these activities are conducted by our fellowmen through organizations and methods that engage the keenest intellects guided by depraved motives and wrecked moral wills. An in-depth knowledge of the nature of the methods and of the blighting results of these institutions of vice is necessary for our better citizens who would eliminate them from civilization. It is this kind of preparedness that the schools the world over should be giving rather than that of military preparedness. This work today is too largely of the form of adult resistance to the enemy of vice that has been systematically bred and nourished in our own homeland. A people will far more quickly recover from the devastation of war than from the devastation of vice. The home and the school should be the point of attack while the present righteous population stands guard.

2. The true idea of government is that of Co-operation

A. The Method of Approach

Children early appreciate what is done for them and learn to enjoy doing things for others. It is in these experiences that the teaching of civics has its beginnings. In other words, it is through the functions of the government and not through the machinery of government that the child learns how to behave, how to obey, serve and respect the individuals and institutions of society. This teaching and instructing will keep the parents, the adults within the bounds of righteousness as well lest they be called hypocrites for not practicing what they preach.

The interests aroused in the small group—the home, school, Temple and community—widen out gradually into the interests of the larger group —the city, state, and nation. This method of approach naturally gives civics a place by the side of other subjects from the first grade on through the entire course of school work.

The formal study of text-books on the machinery of government has not appealed to the interests of children and has not resulted in the awakening of a social consciousness. Children love action and are interested in its results. This is the key to success in civics instruction. Every local unit in group life is the proper text book for this work. Such units are (1) the fire department for protection, (2) the police for safety of property and life, (3) the hospitals for the care of the sick, (4) the streets and roads for service, (5) taxes and rents for the use of property, (6) home and school government, (7) the religious organization, and the many more units that these suggest. The study of these life-units gives an air of simplicity to the teaching of civics that keeps it within the range of the child's experiences and keeps him interested in good government as it touches his own life. This type of concrete work will even be of great value to the pupil that drops out of school along the way and so never reaches the higher grades and the study of formal text-books on civics. In this, he/she can still become a productive member of society.

B. Civics gleans from all other subject lessons

Civics furnishes motivation for all other subjects. The child studies history, geography and other subjects because they interest him in his growth as an individual and as a member of the group. In history he learns what men have done, how they have done it, what mistakes they have made, where they have advanced and where they have hindered human welfare. In geography he learns how people have used the earth to make it feed, clothe and shelter man. In language and grammar he learns how individuals communicate with one another for their pleasure and advancement.

So it is with all other school subjects, the center of their interests is life more abundant. In the furthering of all of these human interests, the practice of social virtues, the observance of rules, regulations and laws, the recognition of inter-state and international rights are every-where apparent. Learning to read is for the double purpose of finding information and joy—both necessary for an efficient citizen. Hence, it is easy and advisable to teach civics in connection with and as a part of all subjects in the curriculum. In a sense, the Holy Koran of the Moorish Science Temple of America exemplifies this necessity as it teaches civics within its pages and has whole chapters dedicated to such.

Keep in mind however, it is also necessary to group together the lessons and principles of civics as they are unfolded in daily life. This unfolding should be analyzed and dissected in the study of the subjects of the school curriculum. Then, the aware teacher can make these lessons the objects of conscious observation and study for moving forward, and lessons to the posterity of the nation. In other words, civics has a content of its own that is both interesting and invaluable and which calls for a separate and continuous treatment in the daily program of the school. It is rich in its significance because it constitutes the vitalizing motive of all school subjects.

C. Civics in the daily life of the child

The importance of the lessons of Civics in the daily life of the child, at every stage of its development and in every human relationship, justifies giving this subject a place of its own in the regular program throughout all of the gradual phases of schooling. It is so recognized in many of the best schools in the United States and foreign countries. In some schools, however, some of the topics necessary for training in citizenship are grouped under the subject of ethics. This seems to be a needless division of subject matter and results in a confusion of emphasis. Ethics should primarily be taught in the Temples or religious organizations and its practice within that individual should automatically lend itself into civic and civil interaction.

The better plan is to keep the instruction closely, but broadly organized under the one subject of civics and citizenship. For instance, the subject of right and duty is just as appropriately called civics as ethics and has a more significant meaning in the term of citizenship, if so designated. Viewing the subject of civics thus broadly, as including all conduct of the individual and the group, we see clearly the necessity for daily attention not only to the practice of civic virtues, but to the interpretation, appreciation and organization of the principles of moral and civic life.

In the Temple's school, this work should be in the form of heart-to-heart talks with the children a few minutes per day, two or three times per week, as the opportunities are offered in connection with the school activities, with the reading and language lessons and with the home and community relations. If your child attends public school, then maybe you can get together with other parents and form study groups around the subject of civics even if they are not interested in Islamic values. Such an education will be vital to the children of your home and others. We must not be afraid to approach other parents with this subject as it is important for teaching those things that will make our people better citizens.

In the intermediate and grammar grades, a regular place on the program should be given two or three days per week for a careful consideration of civic problems through boys' and girls' club work and the various organizations for community life. This should be no less important from teenagers and adults.

The teacher can find much help in the organization of this material in the many elementary books and articles in educational papers that are appearing in the last few years on the subject of civics and citizenship. When the students have an acute understanding of what civics entail, then a simple text, placing the emphasis upon the functioning and machinery of government, should be taught and therefore used by the pupil, in daily study.

A careful organization of the principles of conduct and government should be made around the machinery of government that the state uses to direct and control the life of its citizens. This last course would necessitate the use of a good text-book and it should be closely related to the final survey made in this grade of the history of the United States in general and how it relates to Moorish societies founded under the Islamic spread in the middle ages.

Such a course of instruction will tend to fill society with individuals who know how to and have the habit of governing themselves and who have the knowledge and habit of co-operation with others in government. Legislation will then tend more and more to place its emphasis upon providing the means of correct and universal education and likewise the courts and federal institutions will grow less and less in prominence and consequence.

3. Motivations

On the basis of the child's natural impulse to live and to do something constructive, civics is one of the richest subjects in its appeal to and satisfaction of his/her interests, desires, and aims. The satisfaction found in agreeable, harmonious, and helpful relationships with his/her companions is secured through the observance of regulations and principles that control group life. The child desires the approval of parent and teacher, hence he/she obeys. He/she desires protection; hence he pays his share of the necessary expense. He desires the use of the public highway; hence he observes the laws governing it. He desires to travel abroad or to trade with other nations; hence he acquaints himself with the customs and laws of those nations.

In all of these human relationships he/she is a participant and therefore interested, and concerned with the results. He has these experiences in a concrete way in the groups to which he belongs, thus satisfying his immediate interests or motives. The alert and resourceful teacher finds an abundance of ways in which to stir the child's imagination for the use of these present experiences in his preparation for the future or more remote aims of adult life.

A. Teaching Civics through the Life of the School:

The Temple school must pride itself on being a rich civics laboratory where every child is participating in the exercises and the teacher is creating the environment and conditions favorable to results. The child desires liberty and is taught that he finds it most where order and obedience abounds. He/she learns that industry brings the best rewards. He learns to appreciate good roads and courteous treatment on the way to and from the Temple school. In the various forms of pupil government, literary societies, athletic teams, he learns to co-operate, obey and rule. Through the industrial activities of the Temple group, such as the manual training, cooking and sewing, she learns how the school is served by other institutions in supplying needed materials. Through the Temple's school savings bank, he learns how to co-operate with society in the care and use of wealth. In the use and care of his books and school property he learns the valuable lessons of the use and care of public and private property. In his relation to the school board, the attendance officer, medical director, school nurse, and playground officials he is broadened and enriched in his civic experiences and fitted for the wider life outside of the school. Likewise, his imagination is awakened by the study of the deeds of men in history. The proper utilization of this life of the school is the richest of all civic instruction.

B. Teaching Civics through Local and State Officials and Institutions

The school children are acquainted with local officials, such as road commissioners, village or city councilmen, mayor, policemen, justice of the peace, assessors, the county superintendent of schools, mail carriers and postal clerks. The work of these officials, the children can understand and appreciate because it contributes to their daily life. They will be interested in studying the method of election and/or appointment and control of these officials.

The greater part of the information needed for this work can be obtained by the children from their parents and friends, thus coordinating the school and community interests. The study of the work of these officials and institutions should be approached through concrete problems, such as getting money for public work, keeping the roads in order, adjusting troubles between individuals, sending and receiving mail. In finding the solution to these problems the children receive the desired information and training in citizenship.

C. The City as a Unit in development of Civics Teaching

Because of the rapid development of cities and the great extent to which both city and rural life is controlled by the social and political organizations of the city makes the city a very important unit of civic study. The city government in all of its phases touches not only the life in the home, but is in every essential respect like the government of the state and the nation. It is of greater consequence to the majority of citizens because of the more intimate relations they maintain with the city. And because of this closer intimacy, the problems of social need and control are more concrete and therefore more readily understood and appreciated. Every municipal institution and factory plant may be seen at its work and a first-hand study made of its contribution to the individuals and home of the city.

Such problems as the following open up the study of the entire life of the city: (1) The inspection and care of food, (2) the supply and cost of water, (3) the paving and care of streets and roads, (4) the construction of public utilities, (5) the provision for education, amusement and leisure, (6) the care of the poor, the sick, and the aged, (7) the election, duties and pay of officials, (8) the work of Temples, religious organizations and other types of organizations, (9) the closing of bars, liquor stores, and other dens of vice.

This life-like work through the school gives the pupils a feeling of ownership in the life of the city, and therefore a feeling of personal responsibility for its proper care. This consciousness of responsibility for good government is one of our greatest social needs. It can never be developed through text-book study, but must come through actual participation in civic life.

D. Children enjoy the activities – Teaching Civics through Dramatization

Children enjoy the activities in dramatizing their school lessons and so receive more good from the instruction and drill given them. Much of the work in civics can be made life-like through dramatization. For instance, a number of the pupils may represent the school board, and others, representing parents or agents, may appear before the board in session, on certain business relations pertaining to the school. In this way the pupil may learn of the duties of the board and of their methods of doing business. In a similar way the pupils may dramatize the work of the city council, the justice courts, the directors of a bank, the health department, etc. Having to discharge the duties of the members of these bodies the pupils take more interest and care in posting themselves regarding these duties. As a means of enriching this work, visits should be made to see some of these bodies in session. In each of the play-sessions with the pupils, a real problem in government should be the subject for consideration.

E. Teaching Civics through Community Organization

The most vital training given through the various forms of community organizations in which all members of society are participating.

Illustrations of these organizations are the Parent-Teachers' Associations, the Farmers' Clubs, the Chamber of Commerce, the Moorish Science Temple of America and their Leagues, Churches, Mosques, and Synagogues and their leagues, the Women's Clubs, the Christian Associations like the YMCA.

Most of these organizations are voluntary and exist for civic and religious improvement without pay or legal coercion. The nature and motive of these organizations place them on a high civic plane, making them worthy of observation and study by the school children. Branches of many of these organizations exist for children so that they as members may actually participate in the same character of civic work. These organizations exist primarily for the purpose of awakening, developing and fostering high ideals and practices of civic virtues. They are the forerunners of good laws and law enforcement. They are the foundations and strength of good schools, righteous homes, and spiritual churches. It is through these organizations that the members of a community come to know, love, and co-operate with one another in the work of citizens. This will be the model for the Moorish Science Temple of America as civics is introduced for the first time to the masses of the disenfranchised of this land.

F. Teaching Civics through Holiday Celebrations

Holiday celebrations have for their primary purpose the deepening in the minds of our children and their appreciation of the past heroes and events that have given to us our nationality and its blessings. These celebrations, by their concrete and dramatic method, stir the imaginations of our children to a fuller understanding of the worth of these historic personages and achievements as means of securing the same high type of life today. These appeals to the imagination and the emotions result in a type of patriotism and an impulse to civic service that is of great value in the trials and tests that come to our citizens in critical moments of national life.

Such lessons magnify the ideals of citizenship toward which all civic instruction tends and enriches the aesthetic joy which comes from knowledge of the beauty of unselfish human service.

Such days that we have in this nation been accustomed to such as Christmas, Thanksgiving, Memorial Day, Washington's Birthday, Fourth of July, and many others, are centers around which rich historic memories cluster that fosters themselves within the consciousness of mainly the European Americans of our country. It is no less right that holiday's be established with the same pomp and under the same circumstance that the aforementioned holidays are displayed in this country. Good citizens love these days and our schools do well to help to perpetuate them. All peoples and nations have their festal days. The programs for these celebrations should bring out clearly and simply the true values of the contributions made by the historic heroes and events and not permit these values to be overshadowed by the sensational and transient features of the ceremonies. These exercises offer excellent opportunities for interesting the adult citizens in the work of the schools as well as interesting the children in the work beyond the school.

G. Teaching Civics through Juvenile Leagues

The theory that the child is *father to the man* is recognized in the plan and work of the many Junior Civic Leagues throughout our country. Some of these, such as the Boy Scout Movement and the Camp Fire Girls, have reached great proportions as national organizations.

Their supreme purpose is a clean, happy, useful citizen. The Temples, likewise, have the Young People's Business League and the National Woman's Auxiliary. Such 501 (c) 4 organizations are vital in their function in expressing civic engagement with the community for the youth as they engage in civic and religious work. In some cities there are also Junior Civic and Industrial Leagues working as branches to the Commercial Clubs to train the boys and girls to know, to appreciate and to serve in the industrial life of the cities. The far-reaching significance of this work among the youth cannot be better expressed than by this quotation from the Prophet Noble Drew Ali when he stated:

> *"Look for the best in others and give them the best that is in you. Have a deeper appreciation for womanhood. Brighten the hopes of our youth in order that their courage be increased to dare and do wondrous things. Adhere at all times to the principles of love, truth, peace, freedom, and justice. I am your affectionate leader. I shall continue to labor day and night, both in public and private, for your good, thereby contributing to the welfare of our country and its people as a whole."*

H. Teaching Civics Through Text-books or Online Venues

The old text-books on civics, in which was emphasized the machinery of government, are of but little value, as they fail to interpret to the pupil the facts and relations of his own community life. The newer books of recent years have the "socialized" point of view, and in subject-matter and method, are approaching somewhat nearer to the needs of our purpose. There are several internet sites available that teach detailed civics courses. An online web site or text-book that closes up the previous gap between organized subject-matter and the daily life of the child is a good text for use. There is need for this type of text-book work on civics and citizenship in the upper grades. Such a website or book can well be termed "Community Civics," with the broad conception of community as the group-life throughout the state and nation. In this textbook work emphasis should be placed upon the principles of government as they have been unfolded to the pupils in the concrete work in which they have participated in the lower grades. Likewise a study should be made of the ways in which these principles are applied by our law makers and administrative officials in serving the will of the people. Such a study should have as its ultimate purpose an intelligent initiative on the part of the citizens in the co-operative work of the government as it pertains to human betterment.

The online study or text-book work will secure such results only as it is supplemented and enriched with the methods and devices interpreted and described in the foregoing discussions. Such a course of instruction and training will produce a citizenship capable of maintaining, *"a government of the people, by the people and for the people"*. It is now our turn to re-learn how to run a government.

4. Civics and Citizenship A Course of Study

This syllabus is largely suggestive and should be modified and enlarged by any resourceful teacher and/or Temple group.

A. **Primary phases 1-2- 3:** Duties in the home, school and community
School age children who generally of the first, second and third grades. Adults should master these precepts:

i. *Social Duties*
Kindness, helpfulness, industry, self-respect, unselfishness, co-operation, loyalty, self-control, cleanliness, punctuality, honesty, truthfulness, and social courtesies.

These virtues which are taught in the doctrine of the Moorish Science Temple of America are to be taught in connection with all of the lessons and activities of the school,

ii. *Civic awareness*
Care of life, health and property: How to avoid dangerous animals and vehicles, what to do in case of accidents, CPR training, how to keep well with natural herbs, the care of the eye, ear and throat, how to use and protect one's own and others' property.

These duties are taught in connection with the social and legal regulations governing them.

iii. *How to play and to be happy*

In the group games, in class and on the playground, in the home, in the parks, in sports and other contests, and alone with books, in the garden, field, and woods.

Emphasis is to be placed upon the provisions made by home, school and society for play and joy.

iv. *How to save and invest*
Tomorrow's needs; the Temple or the Temple's school savings bank, the lessons of the community or school garden and the canning clubs, the fishery or the poultry yard and the seed corn, the granary, the store-house of the squirrel, the ant and the bee.

Emphasize the many ways in which society encourages and promotes thrift.

v. *Friendships*
How to make and keep friends; right kind of friends, of people, animals, plants, books, pictures, and ideals.

Stories can be used of great friendships in history by using Koranic and other literature.

vi. *Developing a sound methodology*

The method of civics instruction in the primary grades is always concrete and centers on the lessons and activities of the class room, the school, the street, the highway, the parks, the Temple, the hospitals, libraries, woods and fields.

These lessons create and develop the life and spirit of the individual and the group.

vii. *Holidays and Patriotism* – Using the examples of Thanksgiving, Christmas, Washington's Birthday, Lincoln's Birthday, Fourth of July; Moorish Americans should establish uniform holiday formats and these formats should be followed throughout the nation where members practice the life. Example, the Prophet's birthday, Marcus Garvey's birthday, etc., etc.

These celebrations should consist of simple exercises in which every child can have a part. The aim should be true culturalism and patriotism as a result of an intelligent appreciation of the unselfish service of these heroes and also an awakened desire to do something worthy of appreciation.

viii. *Filial piety*

Reverence: Of parents, self, friends, truth, beauty, work, home, Temple and Allah.

This spirit is the fruitage of all other lessons properly taught. It is the feeling and attitude of mind that nothing shall be permitted to stand between the individual and these objects of reverence.

B. **Fourth Phase**: Continual practice, home and community models, teamwork

    I. *Sustained continuity*

Continuation of the lessons of the primary phases in their broader application to the community and the state. None one in the community should be made to feel that they have outgrown these lessons and its practices.

    II. *The relation of the home to the community*

The right kind of homes, the community institutions that the home needs, such as the market, lighting system, telephones, postal service, fire departments, warehouses, granaries, flour mills, coal mines, lumber yards, parks, hospitals, police departments, religious Temples, libraries.

Theses should he emphasized as supplements to the home and as supported by the co-operative work of the homes. Proper balance should be given to the advantages of both rural and city home in regards to community life. The advantages of each must overshadow the disadvantages to the point that either or can be an acceptable living modality.

    III. *Teamwork in Class, Games and Clubs*

Forms of pupil government, debate teams, athletic contests, basketball, baseball, football, street cleaning brigades, flag drills, fire drills.

In all of this work the emphasis is to be placed upon the importance of co-operation in group life.

C. **Fifth Phase**: The Municipal model
I. *The City—All of its Activities*.
   a) Looking after health.
   b) Inspecting and care of food.
   c) Providing water.
   d) Keeping the city clean and beautiful.
   e) The work of the fire department.
   f) The police department.
   g) The council and the laws.
   h) What the city does for the schools.
   i) Providing recreation and amusements.
   j) How Children's Leagues can help in such work.

II. *The National Community—All of its Activities*.
   a) The school and the problem of consolidation.
   b) Making good roads.
   c) Mail service and telephones.
   d) How farmers are improving their crops and animals.
   e) The problem of health in the nation.
   f) What the county officials do for the people.
   g) What cultural people do for recreation and pleasure.
   h) The opportunity and work of the nation's Temple.
   i) How Boys and Girls Clubs work.

D. **Sixth Phase:** The State model
I. *The State Institutions — All of its institutions*:
   a) The necessity for and the different kinds of schools and reformatory institutions. Show how these mean good citizenship.
   b) Show what the state does through taxes.
   c) Show how the government controls certain kinds of business for the good of the people.
   d) Show what young citizens can do to help the state officials to give the people good government.

   e) Show what the community can do without the state helping.

 II. *Privileges and Duties of Individuals in a State*:

   a) Personal and property rights and duties.

   b) Suffrage rights and duties.

   c) Educational rights and duties.

   d) Military rights and duties.

   e) Religious rights and duties.

   f) Health rights and duties.

   g) Leisure and amusement rights and duties.

E. Seventh phase: Governmental relations with the state and citizens in general

A good text should be studied in this phase.

   a) What the national government does for all citizens.

   b) The rights and duties of all citizens in relation to national government.

   c) How the national government regulates her relations with all citizens.

   d) How each state works with the national government.

   e) How the government gets money.

   f) Who are citizens of the United States and what are their duties. How we make citizens in the Moorish Science Temple of America. How foreigners are made citizens of the United States of America.

   g) How business between the states is regulated.

F. Eighth Phase: Government and state interaction, international relations

A good text should be studied in this phase.

   a) A systematic study of the organization and work of the national, state, county and city governments, through the several departments and officers.

   b) A study of the ways in which the government seeks to equalize responsibilities and blessings.

   c) The mutual relation of the United States and other governments should be made significant through a few type studies; such as, immigration, commerce, travel privileges, studying abroad, religious privileges, intermarriage, and treaties.

5. Conclusion

The Moorish Science Temple of America is a religious organization which first organized as a civic institution. The organization (although the works were/are largely religious), never once lost sight of the fact that the civic side of American life had to be taught to its members and the clean and pure nation of Moors in general. The very words of the founder, Prophet Noble Drew Ali, elucidates this fact.

This guide is merely a compilation of older civics guides that were being taught in the United States in the early 1900's. The reason such an early text was chosen is because it captures the true essence of what civics is without the tainting of what we believe civics is supposed to be about as we are taught today; e.g. big government, crony capitalism, and political posturing. When one understands these basic concepts, then you gain an understanding of what the Prophet meant when he said *"living the life accordingly."*

This early work, published in 1916 entitled *Civics and Citizenship* by David E. Cloyd, was chosen because this compiler felt it best represented Islamism, or more aptly, *Americanized-Islam*. This Americanized Islam is a melding of the new with the old with the certainty that an advancement to the race be made. This guide should be studied intently and applied accordingly. This guide should help the true teacher, meaning one striving to teach those things to make our people better citizens, craft a curriculum that educates and uplifts based on its precepts while juxtaposing its importance with the very moral and self-development lessons found within our Moorish Holy Koran.

Love, Truth, Peace, Freedom & Justice

Sheik Way-El

Who are your local officials?
List their names and telephone numbers

Governor_____

Mayor_____

Sherriff_____

Congressman_____

State representative_____

City Councilman/Ombudsman for your district_____

Police department_____

Public Information office_____

NOTES

NOTES

NOTES

NOTES